BERKHAMSTED

THROUGH TIME

Berkhamsted Local History
& Museum Society

AMBERLEY PUBLISHING

Acknowledgements

Berkhamsted Through Time has been produced by the Berkhamsted Local History & Museum Society, principally by Ken Wallis, assisted by Trisha Wallis, John and Lesley Bradshaw, and Jenny Sherwood, who has checked the text for historical accuracy. It has only been possible thanks to the survival of the work of early local photographers William Claridge, James Thomas Newman, George Henry Sills, and Arthur Henry Hill. The majority of the modern photographs were taken by Ken Wallis; a few recent ones by Eric Holland, Jenny Honour and Trisha Wallis are also included. We have consulted many records including those of Percy Birtchnell, a founder member of the society, who left a considerable archive and who still exerts a great influence on the interpretation of Berkhamsted's history. If we have failed to acknowledge any contributions, we apologise, and likewise for any errors we have overlooked.

This book is dedicated to Les Mitchell
(1929–2012)
Late president of the Berkhamsted Local History & Museum Society
and a lifelong enthusiast of Berkhamsted's local history.

First published 2013

Amberley Publishing
The Hill, Stroud
Gloucestershire, GL5 4EP

www.amberley-books.com

Copyright © Berkhamsted Local History &
Museum Society, 2013

The right of Berkhamsted Local History &
Museum Society to be identified as the Author
of this work has been asserted in accordance with
the Copyrights, Designs and Patents Act 1988.

ISBN 978 1 4456 0901 0

British Library Cataloguing in Publication Data.
A catalogue record for this book is available from
the British Library.

Typeset in 9.5pt on 12pt Celeste.
Typesetting by Amberley Publishing.
Printed in the UK.

Introduction

Berkhamsted, about 30 miles distant from London, is a linear town set in the valley of the River Bulbourne. Today little more than a stream, this river once flowed strongly enough to power two water mills, the Upper and Lower Mill, both mentioned in the Domesday Book. The name is Saxon and means 'a homestead among the hills', or 'homestead among the birches'. Trees are still very much a feature of the town's landscape today. The High Street follows much the same route as the Roman Akeman Street. South of the High Street, roads with mostly Victorian houses rise steeply from the valley bottom. On the other side, where there were once water meadows, the valley broadens out to make room for the canal (1798) and the railway (1837). Beyond stands the Norman castle (1067), the best-preserved motte-and-bailey castle remaining in the country. Behind the castle are roads of later twentieth-century housing, climbing up the hill towards the common and the open countryside beyond. Berkhamsted is a market town, its trading rights dating back to the time of Edward the Confessor.

This valley was settled from very early times. Archaeological evidence of Neolithic, Iron Age, Roman and Saxon dates are proof of this. Immediately before the Norman Conquest, Edmar, a thane under Harold, controlled Berkhamsted and the surrounding area. After the defeat of Harold at Hastings, Duke William marched through the south of England, pillaging as he went. He crossed the Thames at Wallingford and reached Berkhamsted. Here he was met by Edgar Atheling, Archbishop Aldred, the Earls Edwin and Morcar and the chief men of London, who offered him the crown in return for good government.

William granted the manor and honour of Berkhamsted to his half-brother, Count Robert of Mortain, and instructed him to erect a motte-and-bailey castle as part of the defence of the route to London. The first castle was a timber structure with a double moat. This was later replaced by a stone structure, the ruins of which remain today. The castle has many royal associations, was part of the Earldom and then later the Duchy of Cornwall. Richard, Earl of Cornwall, made Berkhamsted his administrative centre for the Earldom. The Black Prince, the first Duke of Cornwall, spent his honeymoon here, and the park was also his favourite hunting ground. In 1216 the castle was besieged by Prince Louis of France, and later King John of France was imprisoned here after being captured by the Black Prince at the battle of Poitiers. Cicely, Duchess of York, mother of Richard III and grandmother of the princes in the Tower, was the last resident of the castle. Since her death in 1495 the castle has belonged to the Duchy of Cornwall. Even in its ruined state it has witnessed many important events.

While the castle flourished, Berkhamsted benefited from the extra trade arising from the needs of the royal household. After its demise Berkhamsted initially felt the loss of this extra status and also suffered from the granting of a royal charter to Hemel Hempstead by Henry VIII, but Tudor times saw the foundation of Berkhamsted School (1541), the building of the Court House and the construction of Berkhamsted Place, largely from the ruins of the castle. During the Civil War, Berkhamsted, like most of Hertfordshire, supported Cromwell, and the Murrays at Berkhamsted Place, staunch Royalists, were dispossessed. The Cromwellian Daniel Axtell lived there until he was executed as a regicide at the Restoration, when the Murrays were reinstated.

In the eighteenth century the strategic position of Berkhamsted on the route from London to Birmingham and the north put the town once more on the map. In July 1762 the Sparrows Herne Turnpike Trust held its first meeting in the Kings Arms. The Trust became responsible for the 27 miles of highway from Bushey Heath to Aylesbury, via Watford, Berkhamsted and Tring. In the heyday of coaching, services ran several times a week between London, Banbury and Birmingham and Kidderminster.

In spite of the building of several larger houses in the High Street and some on the outskirts, Berkhamsted as it had been in medieval times had changed very little. It was still clustered round the High Street, Castle Street, Chesham Road and Water Lane. Leading off the High Street were several little yards containing cottages. The topography had not changed.

The coming of the Grand Junction Canal, opened through Berkhamsted in 1798, and the London & Birmingham Railway in 1837, brought not only an increase in prosperity with the growth of new industry but extreme overcrowding in the narrow alleys in the town centre. There was an urgent need for housing. This was gradually met from the 1850s onwards by the sale of land from some of the larger houses.

The manor and honour of Berkhamsted remained part of the Duchy of Cornwall, but in 1761 the Duchy leased the manor to the Duke of Bridgewater at Ashridge. In 1863 Lord Brownlow's trustees bought the whole of the manor, with the exception of the castle, from the Duchy. Economic pressures and the legacy of two World Wars in the twentieth century accelerated the break-up of large estates, thus providing land for further housing. The closure of many industrial firms in the town centre in the second half of the twentieth century equally changed the nature of the town.

In spite of the increase in size, especially during the last forty years, and the large number of people commuting to London, Berkhamsted remains a thriving community, surrounded by fine countryside. In this selection of photographs we have attempted to show the changes that have taken place since the mid-nineteenth century. A great deal has had to be left out, but we hope that we have given you an impression of our historic market town.

The Old Mill

Situated at the junction of the High Street and Bank Mill Lane, the Old Mill House lies next to the River Bulbourne. Two mills are mentioned in the Domesday Book but are not distinguishable. It is believed that Upper Mill (in Mill Street) may have its origins in the ninth century. In the accounts of the Earldom of Cornwall at the end of the thirteenth century, Bank Mill is identified by name. It operated as a mill until its closure in 1900, since when it has been a hotel, public house and now a restaurant. An archaeological survey was undertaken and substantial remains of the mill race and wheel pit still survive.

The Hall, Berkhamsted. Towards Boxmoor.

The Hall I

Until 1937, the first house one saw on the south side of the High Street on entering the town from the east would have been a large forbidding building called the Hall. Nestling behind a high brick wall, the rather gaunt, grey, three-storey Georgian building was set in magnificent gardens. In the late eighteenth century it was home to the Receiver General of the Post Office Augustus Pechell and his wife Sarah, but over the years it passed through several owners. In 1917 Edward Greene, brother of the headmaster of the Berkhamsted School, C. H. Greene, owned the house. It was purchased by Berkhamsted School in May 1928 and used as a preparatory school until 1937, when it was then demolished.

The Hall II

The building fronted onto extensive grounds of some 25 acres. The gardens were magnificent, with many greenhouses and numerous mature trees. The interior contained many handsome rooms, such as the entrance hall seen in the lower picture. In 1851 it was home to Thomas Halsey, a Member of Parliament, who employed a significant number of local residents as indoor staff, gardeners and labourers. At the sale in 1937 the grounds were purchased for housing development and became the Hall Park estate. New road names reflected the estate's history. Greene Walk recalled its owner from 1917, and Cedar Road and Cedar Way recall the magnificent tree that grew in the grounds. Hall Park, Hall Park Hill, Hall Park Gate and Upper Hall Park all recognise the estate itself.

HIGH ST. BERKHAMSTED LOOKING FROM "THE HALL."   SILLS, Photo.

First View of the High Street

The first view of the High Street is shown in this early George Sills photograph, with the walls of the Hall on the left and the start of the cottages lining both sides of the road. The Hall has now been replaced by Swing Gate School at the corner of Swing Gate Lane. In 1762 the High Street became part of the Sparrow Herne Turnpike Trust. This ran from Bushey Heath through Watford, Berkhamsted, and Tring to the outskirts of Aylesbury. The first meeting of the trustees was at the Kings Arms in July 1762, and many further meetings were held there. The Trust continued until 1 November 1873 and brought much prosperity to the town.

G. Pearce, Newsagent

Many of the cottages lining the High Street not only provided living accommodation for the residents but also their place of employment. Many turned their front rooms into sales premises. Situated on the south side of the road, G. Pearce was a newsagent, tobacconist, confectioner and general store. Delivery of goods was aided by the tricycle with a box on the front. The trade may have changed over the years but the buildings are recognisably the same.

Pocock's Forge

Before the coming of motor transport, the horse was the main motive power and each one needed shoeing on a regular basis. One of the best-known families in the town was the Pocock family, several generations of which have been blacksmiths. These photographs show views of the forge situated on the south side of the road. By 1900 Charles and Frank Pocock had branched out and become engineers and the lower view shows the family with some of the items that the forge would have produced.

McIntyre House

One of the most important businesses, and possibly the largest employer in its heyday, was the chemical works of William Cooper, which produced sheep dip. From his arrival in Berkhamsted around 1843, the firm spread along the High Street and down Ravens Lane and Manor Street. By 1959 the company had been acquired by the Wellcome Foundation. In 1995 the Berkhamsted factory became part of the chemical combine Agr-Evo UK. The building known as McKintyre House was used as offices until that firm closed in July 1997; the site is now new housing.

Callaghan's Garage

In the 1933 edition of Kelly's Directory, George Callaghan is advertising as a motor haulage and general cartage contractor at 33 High Street. Following the Second World War he was operating a petrol garage and motor repair shop. Although the garage has gone, the site maintains the name as Callaghan Court.

East's Woodyard

Looking back towards Pocock's forge there is a row of cottages which was where Job East had his first timber yard before Callaghan's garage was built. The building in the centre of the photograph was the Black Horse public house but is now the Curry Garden Indian restaurant.

Holliday's Bicycle Shop

On the opposite side of the road there is a shop that began as a wheelwright's, run by John Holliday and his family, and which can be traced back to before 1840. The family progressed through pedal cycles to motorcycles. Although the shop business has changed several times since, the family name is still recorded in the road that runs off the High Street.

The Poplars

As the sheep dip business expanded, William Cooper moved from the small cottage in Castle Street into the house on the south side of the High Street called the Poplars, visible on the extreme left of the picture. He died there in May 1885. Later it was the birthplace of the actor Sir Michael Hordern. Latterly the coach house of the Poplars was demolished to provide a road entrance to the new houses built on the extensive land behind the house.

Egerton House

A property that no longer exists was a sixteenth-century building called Egerton House. This two-storey building, which had attics above, had a coarse rendered elevation that was divided at the first-floor level by a wood string course. The roof was tiled and at each end of the house there was a projecting chimney stack. The house fronted onto the High Street with three projecting bays; above each was a gable.

Inside Egerton House
The interior had been considerably restored but it had retained some of the original fireplaces, some of the old oak beams and the doors. J. M. Barrie was a regular visitor during the residence of the Llewellyn-Davies family, on whose children *Peter Pan* was based. It is believed that there was a private performance in the house of *Peter Pan* when one of the children was ill. When the *Inventory of the Monuments of Hertfordshire* was written in 1911, the building was reported to be in good condition, but it only lasted until 1938, when it was demolished.

The Rex Cinema

A cinema and a parade of shops replaced Egerton House. The cinema had risen in popularity following the Second World War, but with the advent of television it began to wane. The Rex cinema struggled on until it closed in 1973, and was left boarded up. Around the country many cinemas were being demolished, so an effort was made to preserve a few examples. In 1988 the building was accorded listed building status for its David Nye interior, becoming the only cinema in Hertfordshire to achieve such an accolade. The parade of shops was converted into housing and the cinema was renovated. The entrance foyer, with its stylish Art Deco interior, was converted into The Gatsby. Both are popular venues.

The Co-op Society

Berkhamsted & District Co-operative Society started with a number of small shops at various locations in the town. These prospered and developed into three substantial buildings. This one was at the corner of Manor Street. Figgs the chemist was at 173 High Street until 2003; the name is now perpetuated in the pharmacy in this building.

Church und High Street Berkhamstedt

Pilkington Manor I

This early postcard of St Peter's church and the High Street looking towards the west was printed in Frankfurt, Germany, which accounts for the use of 'und', the German word for 'and', and for the spelling of 'Berkhamstedt'. It was common for early photographers in this country to have their postcards produced in Germany. Arthur Henry Hill was born in St Pancras in 1869 and in the 1901 census he was described as a brewer's clerk living at 236 High Street. In 1902 he is described as a fancy goods and toy dealer, but he has left Berkhamsted by 1904. During his stay in Berkhamsted is when he is likely to have produced his postcards. George Henry Sills ran a successful business and counted royalty and members of the landed gentry among his clientele. He secured commissions from Queen Victoria, Edward VII and George V as well as Lord Brownlow, amongst others.

HIGH STREET, BERKHAMSTED.   G.H. SILLS Photo.

Pilkington Manor II

Pilkington Manor is first mentioned in the seventeenth century, although it may be earlier, but the building shown here is an eighteenth-century replacement. The extensive estate that went with the house was sold off piecemeal during the nineteenth century. By 1890 the Manor House had been turned into three dwellings. This photograph, taken around 1949, shows the house in a sorry state, and the building was demolished soon after and a row of shops built. Today they have gone and a row of flats now occupy the site, which bears the title Pilkington Manor that is incorporated into a copy of the original doorway.

St Peter's Church

The parish church of St Peter's sits in the heart of the town. For convenience 1222 is suggested as the date of consecration, as in that year Robert de Tuardo was instituted as the first recorded rector. Over time the fabric has been much altered. A much-criticised restoration was carried out by Jeffry Wyattville who covered the church with Stucco, which looked tawdry. William Butterfield re-faced the exterior with the present flint-work in 1870 and filled in the door to the parish fire engine, which was at the south-west corner of the church.

Inside St Peter's Church
The wall above the chancel arch was decorated with a religious scene depicting the Ascension. It was painted in 1872 as a gift from Sophia Jane Hutchinson in memory of her husband, the Revd James Hutchinson, who was the rector 1851–71. It was obliterated during the redecoration some time during the 1960s. Jeffry Wyattville started the interior clearance, which has continued with the re-siting of the vestry and the Torrington Tomb. The building has been adapted to fulfil the needs of the ever-changing congregation.

The Court House

Next to St Peter's church is the Court House. Another sixteenth-century building, it was originally of two floors with an attic storey. The ground floor has been re-faced with brick and flint, and the projecting upper storey is of timber. The floor to the attic storey has been removed to reveal the timber roof and there are still some impressive beams, which had supported the floor of the loft. The Borough Court used to be held in this building, which later became a church school. At the other end of Church Lane is another surviving small building, which has had many uses and now houses a hair salon.

Back Lane

The small lane behind Grab-All Row was originally called Back Lane but is now referred to as Church Lane. It contained a number of ancient houses. This building survived as it was used as workshops and later as a store for Neil's furniture store, before being converted into two desirable properties. Together with The Wilderness and Water Lane, this area developed an unsavoury nature with the Locke & Smith brewery, the earliest gasworks, the Baptist burial ground and slaughterhouses.

For Photographs

OF ALL KINDS, GO TO
THE OLDEST HOUSE
AND ESTABLISHMENT
IN THE TOWN.

J. T. NEWMAN,

The Art Studio, Incents House,
Berkhamsted.　　Telephone No. 17.

J. T. Newman, Photographer

It is to James Newman that we must be grateful for many of the views of Berkhamsted. Born in Wilstone in 1860, his father was a wheelwright, a career in which James showed no interest. He trained as a photographer at Piggot's in Leighton Buzzard and came to Berkhamsted around 1888. His first studio was at 176 High Street, and he moved to Dean Incent's House around 1907/08. The photograph of Newman shows him with the compact portable camera of the day. Between 1930 and 1970 the house was used as a charming old-world tea shop and restaurant.

Dean Incent's House

This much-restored sixteenth-century house is said to have been the home of John Incent, founder of Berkhamsted School, who became Dean of St Paul's Cathedral. His father Robert Incent was a wealthy townsman and secretary to Cicely, Duchess of York, who resided at the castle. Robert died in 1485 when John was about five years old. Traditionally his arms as Dean have been hung outside the house.

The Swan Hotel

The seventeenth-century Swan Hotel is no longer a drinking establishment but is now the base for the Swan Youth Project, which provides accommodation for young people and facilities for the youth of the town. It stands at the corner of what is now Chesham Road but was previously called Grubs Lane and originally Elvyne Lane. Further along, the Crown is still an active public house and restaurant, and on the opposite side of the road are the shops of Grab-All Row. The road is not that busy, reflecting a quiet rural market town.

Changing Transport

This busy Edwardian photograph shows the principal mode of transport, the horse and cart. With no Highway Code and a lack of motor transport, people congregate down the middle of the road. Unlike our predecessors, who mostly walked, it seems the modern shopper has to use a car. Car parking is now the highest priority in the town centre, which has caused the thoroughfare to be narrowed so that shoppers can park their cars close to the shops.

The High Street I

By the mid-1950s the motor car was beginning to make its mark; not a horse in sight. A car was expensive to purchase so it was considered to be a luxury item, but delivery vans were becoming the norm. The shops and public houses have changed very little and the scene is still recognisable today. Brandon & Son furnishers and Castle & Co. Ltd wine and spirit merchants next door are the noticeable buildings.

Grab-All Row

This nineteenth-century photograph shows the shops at the eastern end of Grab-All Row. Two names can be identified: Baldwin and Fenner. In Kelly's Directory of 1862, and the census returns for 1871 and 1881, Henry Baldwin is recorded as a baker, and Henry Fenner as a hairdresser and perfumer. Neither is recorded here in the 1891 census. The old grapevine that can be seen growing up the front of Fenner's shop can still be seen, and the shop is still a barber's today.

The Court Theatre I

We can now see the view of Grab-All Row looking eastwards. The One Bell public house sign hangs from the building immediately behind the 'keep left' sign. New buildings are evident, including the Home & Colonial Stores that hides the church tower (now the Home & Colonial antique emporium), which as you can see from the photograph on page 30 was Brandon's and later Neil's furniture store. To the left stands the Court Theatre at the corner of Water Lane and Back Lane.

The Court Theatre II

The Court Theatre was built as a picture playhouse and used for entertaining men from the Inns of Court Regiment, stationed in Berkhamsted during the First World War. The first performance was in March 1917, and over the years many amateur theatricals were performed here. In 1934 it was refurbished to increase the seating capacity, before closing at Easter, 1960. It was then bought and used by Tesco. Following a disastrous fire in 1969 the site was cleared and a new Tesco built. It is now called a Tesco Metro. The One Bell public house was demolished in 1959 and replaced by a Victoria Wine off-licence, which is now part of Aitchison's Estate Agents.

The King's Arms

The King's Arms is the most important of the three public houses in this row. Originally a coaching inn, it offered stabling for forty horses, and dates from the reign of Queen Anne. Much of the business of the town was transacted within this building. In 1833 a meeting to protest against the building of the railway and the auction of some of the principal houses were the type of business held here. John Page was the innkeeper here between 1792–1840, and it was during this period that it was a regular venue for the liaison between his daughter, Polly, and King Louis XVIII of France while he was in exile in Hartwell House near Aylesbury.

The Waitrose Site

On the opposite side of Water Lane stood the offices of Locke & Smith, one of the local brewers, and their works extended down Water Lane. The firm was taken over by Benskins of Watford before being closed down shortly before the First World War. The building was being used by Kepston's pulley works when it was burnt down in 1929. Following extensive redevelopment in the 1970s Woolworth's and the Waitrose supermarket occupied the site.

The Waitrose Mural

When Waitrose moved to its current site in December 1996, the frontage of the old shop was boarded up and a mural was painted to cover the bare wood. Local schools were involved in painting the mural with a canal theme. It seemed to deter the vandals, graffiti artists and bill posters and added a decorative element to the empty building.

Civic Centre

The Local Government Act 1888 caused the Berkhamsted Urban District Council to come into being in 1898. Not having a Civic Centre, the council met for the first few years in the boardroom of the workhouse. Eventually they acquired the premises of William Nash & Sons, Builders and Contractors. This 1935 photograph shows the council office and yard, next door to H. Truman & Co., electrical, radio, and refrigerating engineers, light and power contractors. The bunting celebrates the Silver Jubilee of King George V and Queen Mary. This building was demolished in 1937 and the new Civic Centre was built. Walter Pitkin JP, chairman of the Urban District Council, laid the foundation stone and the building was opened in 1938.

The High Street from St Peter's Church Tower

This later view gives a panorama of the High Street. Norman Clarke Ltd replaces H. Truman, and the Dwight Brothers, motor engineers, are still here from before the First World War. The premises of Hubert Figgs chemist's are prominent. Next door is Penny & Thorne solicitors', which is still there today. The substantial building in the middle of the photograph, which became the Hertfordshire Adult Education Centre and is currently occupied by Bet Fred, was previously the Star Tea Co. Ltd (tea merchants) which then became the Star Supply Stores.

Town Hall

Berkhamsted is a market town and animals were traded in temporary pens in front of the Town Hall. The cattle market was on alternate Wednesdays, with a straw plait market held every Thursday and a miscellaneous market every Saturday. This distinctive building was built in 1859 and opened in 1860 following a competition that was won by Edward Buckton Lamb. The market rights, which were vested in the owners of Ashridge House, were acquired by the Town Hall Committee for a nominal sum after the First World War. The White Hart can be seen to the right of the Town Hall and the waterworks beyond that.

The Mechanics' Institute

The distinctive design of the Town Hall was the subject of a competition which was won by Edward Buckton Lamb and was paid for by public subscription. It cost £3,291 with additional monies being needed for the furnishings. It was opened in August 1860, almost six years after the old market house had burned down. In 1890 the Sessions Hall and the Mechanics' Institute billiard room were added. Until the Civic Centre was built Local Council meetings and the Magistrates' Court met here, and amateur dramatics, exhibitions, dinners and dances and other social events were hosted in the Great Hall.

The popular countrywide movement of the Mechanics' Institute had reached Berkhamsted in 1845. At that time a reading room was established in the house of Mr Platrier, whilst the first lectures were held in a room in the Grammar School. When the Town Hall was planned it was to accommodate a market house and adequate accommodation for the Mechanics' Institute. As soon as the reading room and library were established evening classes were started to encourage further education in the local population. The term 'Mechanics' was dropped from the title in 1930 and the Berkhamsted Institute was finally wound up in April 1993.

The Market

The market is probably the town's oldest institution. In 1217 the market day in Berkhamsted changed from Sunday to Monday, and there was considerable rivalry between the local market towns. The prosperity of the town steadily declined with the decay of the castle. In the reign of Elizabeth I the inhabitants built a market house at the top of Water Lane, which stood until it burnt down in 1854. The ground floor of the Town Hall was the market house replacement. It later accommodated a group of small shops, which have now closed, and the area has been occupied by a succession of cafés and restaurants. The street market held on a Saturday has become more popular. There are now an additional Wednesday and several Sunday markets. These street traders now provide much-needed financial support to the Town Hall Trust.

Figg's the Chemist

Hubert Figg passed the pharmacy examination and was registered as a 'Chemist and Druggist' on 8 July 1912. At that time his registered address was given as 262 High Street, but he moved to 145 High Street in 1921 (High Street was renumbered in 1950 and the building became number 173). He remained here until he ceased being the proprietor of the pharmacy during 1965. The pharmacy name has been retained, but it moved in 2000 to 112 High Street and then again in 2002 to 90 High Street, where it remains today (see page 19). Hubert Figg died in 1982.

When 173 High Street was being renovated it was found that behind the Victorian frontage there was an old timber-framed house. Dendochronology dated the timbers to between 1277 and 1297, and it was part of a box-framed open hall with a crown post and walls of wattle and daub. The building had been considerably altered during its lifetime, but mostly during the seventeenth century. Following its restoration, the ground-floor shop is now occupied by Claire Lloyd properties.

Loosley & Sons

George Loosley was born in Alscot, Princes Risborough, in 1834. By 1861, aged twenty-six, he had become a British Schoolmaster in Buckinghamshire. He married Charlotte Jane Kerry in 1862 and by 1871 they had moved to Berkhamsted. In 1881 he opened a shop in Castle Street as a newsagent and stationer; he also became a journalist for the *West Herts Observer*. By 1901 his children seem to have been running his business interests, as he was only recorded as Superintendent Registrar. The new shop at 176–178 High Street was first recorded in an Almanac of 1909 published by Loosley. By this time G. Loosley & Sons had branched out into printing, publishing and running a servants' registry. He founded the *Berkhamsted Times* in 1875, and the *Berkhamsted Almanack and Directories* was published regularly. He was also the official printer to the Inns of Court Officer Training Corps when it was based in the town during the First World War. In 1909 George and Charlotte were living in Bay House in Charles Street, which is where Bay Court can now be found. The family were involved in the local Baptist church, where George was church secretary from 1878 to 1905. The family presented two new hymn boards and one of the sons, Raymond, presented a pulpit Bible to the church.

The Police Station

In 1764 T. H. Boyes was instructed by the Justices of the Peace to find a suitable place for use as a bridewell. He favoured converting existing tenements at the junction of Bridewell Lane (which later became Kings Road) and the High Street. Although the Justices had reservations about the suitability of the property, it was not until 1894 that the old Bridewell was demolished and a new police station was erected on the site. The Victorian building lasted until 1972, when it was demolished and a new one erected. In 2012 the police moved out of the purpose-built station and moved into accommodation in the Civic Centre. Now if you need a policeman you need to use the telephone.

The High Street II

Here is another mid-1950s view, this time of the junction of the High Street and Lower Kings Road. The buildings have not changed much, although their occupants have changed several times in the intervening years.

Pike's Corner

Lower Kings Road was built in 1885 in order to provide a more direct route to the railway station for the residents at the south-west end of town who commuted to London. The money was raised by public subscription. At the junction the corner shop became known as Pike's corner, in memory of Mr David Pike, a greengrocer who had traded there since 1895. It remained a greengrocer's for many years and local residents will remember buying their vegetables from the display, which expanded onto the pavement. On the other corner there was Edward Henry Morris & Sons, who were a watch and clockmaker's. Redeveloped in 1933, it has since been a tobacconist, a bookshop, fishmonger and now a sandwich shop. The clock dial below the cupola records a local watchmaker, jeweller and engraver, E. C. de Lisle, who had premises at 2/4 Lower Kings Road.

Sharland's Shop

William Jack Sharland opened his draper's shop at the corner of Elm Grove just before the Second World War. The shop was quite small so he later moved to larger premises across the road. P. C. Birtchnell moved from his first shop, in the parade of shops attached to the Rex cinema, into Sharland's old premises. In 1978 a film crew arrived at the premises to make a film of *The Human Factor* by Graham Greene. Based on the spy novel which was partly set in Berkhamsted, it featured Nicol Williamson, Iman, Derek Jacobi, John Gielgud, Ann Todd, Robert Morley and Richard Attenborough. This photograph shows the boy Sam waiting to go into Birtchnell's to buy his school uniform.

Birtchnell's Shop

The substantial building of three floors had been sold in 2010 and left empty over a cold wet winter. In the early hours of Sunday 30 January 2011 the front of the building collapsed into the road in front. Fortunately nobody was under the fallen masonry but it caused chaos for the whole day while workmen shored up the remaining building. The building was declared unsafe and during the following week its demolition was completed.

From an early age Percy Charles Birtchnell was interested in local history. He regularly wrote articles for the local newspapers, contributing to the *Berkhamsted Gazette* and the *Watford Observer*. He also contributed weekly articles to the trade magazines the *Draper's Record* and *Men's Wear*. He is probably best known for his contributions to the *Berkhamsted Review* where he used the pen name of Beorcham (an early spelling for Berkhamsted). He wrote and published a *Short History of Berkhamsted* in 1960, which was republished, in an enlarged and revised edition, in 1972. He also wrote *Bygone Berkhamsted* and booklets on the history of the Town Hall and the Mechanics' Institute. His interest in local history led him, with other like-minded people, to form the Berkhamsted & District Local History Society and he became their Honorary Secretary. Percy died on 12 March 1986 after suffering a heart attack, but the shop continued to trade, with Bob Clark in charge, until its sale in 2010.

Elm Grove House

On the opposite side of Elm Grove there originally stood a similar, substantial building to Birtchnell's. This was called Elm Grove House and in 1898 Sidney Algernon Bontor and Frederick Charles Simpson, surgeons, held their surgery here. It later became the dental surgery of Nico Hofmeyr Bartmann and then Claude Pocock. The building was later demolished and the site is now occupied by the Nationwide Building Society and Ash hairdressing salon. There is still a public telephone box on the pavement, although it is not the 1935 K6 type phone box based on a design by Giles Gilbert Scott; instead it has been replaced by a modern design. An example of the earlier type of phone box is situated on the pavement opposite St Peter's church, which is a listed structure within the conservation area.

H. C. Ward & Son

The 1898 Kelly's Directory proudly advertises Humphrey Charles Ward & Son as 'drapers, silk mercers, hosiers and hatters, French stays, baby linen, millinery, mantles, carpets etc.' Founded in 1790, his shop ultimately extended from 188–194 High Street. William Sharland moved his emporium from across the road to these larger premises, and in the 1960s the firm financed a substantial redevelopment behind the eastern most part of the building. The original roof timbers were included in the rebuilding.

Mackays

These premises remain much the same today as they did after William Sharland's redevelopment, but Mackays replaced Sharland's and they in turn have been replaced by M&Co. However, the type of merchandise that is sold by the occupiers has changed very little over the 200-year life of the buildings.

The Bourne School

Looking back towards the church, this turn-of-the-century view shows the Bourne School. Founded by the generous benefactor, Thomas Bourne, the school opened in 1737 and provided free tuition and uniforms, plus a shilling per week for the parents, for twenty boys and ten girls. The building was extended to provide a new schoolroom at the rear of the building in 1853, funded by public subscription. The next year General John Finch of Berkhamsted Place financed the rebuilding of the original school building because of its dilapidated state. In 1875 all the children were incorporated into the National School. The building was used by the Berkhamsted Girls' School from its founding in 1888, before becoming a branch of the National Provincial Bank in 1902. The Britannia Building Society now resides in the building. The three coats of arms above the door are, from left to right, the arms of Thomas Bourne, Berkhamsted Town and General Finch.

The Co-op Society Offices

Built in 1933, this building started out as the Berkhamsted & District Co-operative Society Ltd registered offices. We have already seen their number one branch at the corner of Manor Street (see page 19). The building has now been sub-divided into three smaller shops, but otherwise the façade has not changed significantly.

Pethybridge Carriages

Before the advent of the motor car, horse-drawn carriages were the norm. One of the carriage manufacturers in Berkhamsted was John Pethybridge. This late nineteenth-century photograph shows a selection of his carriages outside his premises. He died in 1887 and he is buried, with his wife and sons who all predeceased him, in Rectory Lane Cemetery. Who knows if any of his carriages survive today? His premises have been completely replaced by this new building.

Co-op
At the bottom of Cowper Road (Nos 32–33) were the buildings which housed the Berkhamsted & District Co-operative Society. The manager lived next door at No. 34 Cowper Road. A block of flats and a car park now occupy the site.

Sayer's Almshouses

Although John Sayer was cook to Charles II, he had private means and he took a lease on Berkhamsted Place. He died in Berkhamsted in 1682 and has a memorial in St Peter's church. In his will, dated 1681, he bequeathed £1,000 for the building of almshouses and the relief of the poor of the parish. Unfortunately he had not prepared a scheme before he died, which left his wife to implement the terms of the will. She survived him by thirty years and not only drew up an elaborate set of instructions for the trustees to follow but added to the endowment. The almshouses provided twelve rooms for six poor widows, who had each lived in the parish for at least ten years. They had to be frequenters of divine service, as set by the Church of England, and aged at least fifty-five years. The building cost £269 and the balance of the fund was invested, with the annual income devoted to the needs of the almswomen and other poor of the parish.

Great Berkhamsted Gas, Light & Coke Company

Next door to the almshouses was the Royal Oak beer house. The last proprietor was Joseph Batchelor when the building was demolished in 1909. The Great Berkhamsted Gas Light & Coke Company built the first gasworks in 1849, in the Wilderness, where the Water Lane car park is today. By the end of the century the number of complaints about the works being in the centre of the town was rising, so the works moved to land at Billet Lane, between the railway and canal. New offices were built on the site of the Royal Oak. The company became part of the Eastern Gas Board, as a result of the Gas and Coal Act 1948, and the building housed a showroom. It is now a restaurant.

Lane's Nursery

Here we have a George Sills photograph looking back towards the town centre. Henry Lane founded his nurseries here in 1777. This site became the Home Nursery and by 1851 the firm had built large greenhouses on either side of St John's Well Lane, stretching back to the River Bulbourne. As the firm prospered it acquired further land at Potten End and at Broadway. The nursery was famous for selling an apple tree called 'Lane's Prince Albert'. The originator of the tree was Thomas Squire, who lived at the Homestead further back along the High Street. He planted a tree in his garden which he named the Victoria and Albert, and it produced excellent fruit. The saplings were grown and marketed by Lane's Nurseries, with the name changed to reflect his business.

James Wood & Sons

When James Wood came to Berkhamsted he lived in Monks Cottage and set up his Iron Works next door. James Wood & Sons advertised themselves as 'iron fence makers, wire workers & hot water engineers' and they produced a wide range of ironware. James Wood died in 1861 and his widow continued the business for some time after. Eventually the nature of the business changed to a thriving plant nursery and giftware shop before being bought out by Capital Gardens Ltd, but it is still marketed under the name of Woods Gift & Garden Centre. The glazed iron framed building was destroyed by fire in 1974.

Post Office

Built on the site of Lane's Home Nursery, this large 1950s building housed the post office counter, fronting onto the High Street, with the sorting office behind. The latter continued here until 2011, while the post office counter moved along the street to share a shop with the Way Inn. A parcel collection office remained on the site until the sorting office moved to Maylands Avenue, Hemel Hempstead, in 2011.

Edwin King & Sons

This early twentieth-century view, taken by George Henry Sills, shows the other local coachbuilder, Edwin King & Sons. Sidney King lived next door to the Quaker Meeting house and the works were next door at 235 High Street. When the Kings' works closed in 1937, the builder and contractor Donald Lockhart took over the site. The solicitors Sumner & Tabor have their premises here today. Standing alongside the motor car is the chauffeur dressed in his smart uniform with peaked cap and leather boots. This makes quite a contrast to the horse-drawn wagon in the background.

Venetian Villas

Between Sumner & Tabor and Kitsbury Road there is a group of three small shops. Again, although the buildings have not changed significantly the businesses have. What is now the dental surgery has been a dress shop, a fishmonger's and later a butcher's. In 1904 the middle shop, the Venetian Villas, was home to Thomas Gayton, a hairdresser, and the end shop was a bootmaker before becoming a men's hairdresser.

H. E. West's Boot and Shoe Shop

At the beginning of the twentieth century H. E. West ran a boot and shoe shop on the corner of Kitsbury Road. The shop window is full of his goods and presumably it is Mr West standing in the doorway with a string of boots hanging either side of him. The building is now a bed and breakfast and a café with internet access on the ground floor. On the other side of Kitsbury Road stood the Union's second workhouse which was built in 1831; it closed in 1935. The inmates transferred to Hemel Hempstead, and the building was demolished in 1937. A parade of shops now stands on the site.

Primitive Methodist Church

On the opposite side of the High Street stood the Primitive Methodist church. Methodism came to Berkhamsted in the early nineteenth century and the early meetings were held in local cottages before the use of Egerton House was obtained for a short time. A Wesleyan church was built in Highfield Road in 1854 but was only used for two years. The Primitive Methodist group then met in a house in Castle Street until sufficient funds were obtained to build this edifice in 1867. The Primitive Methodists became a dominant force within the town with a substantial congregation. With the amalgamation of the various sub-groups, the independent buildings became superfluous. Since 9 April 1976 the Anglican and Methodist communities have shared All Saints church. This building was redeveloped to provide office accommodation and named Marlowe House. Latterly the upper floors were converted into flats and a Domino's takeaway pizza opened.

Underhill & Young Motor Engineers

On the opposite side of Park Street there is now an outlet of National Tyre & Autocare. This corner premises was once the garage of Underhill & Young Motor Engineers. There were pumps in front of the building just behind the pedestrian pavement. Against the wall, underneath the window to the left of the waiting room door, is a large, painted iron post that recalls the name of the Sparrow Herne Turnpike Trust. Again the occupants of the buildings have changed whereas the buildings have not.

Dealey's Motor Repair Works

This is now in the area called Gossoms End, a suburb of Berkhamsted. Towards Billet Lane there is a small parade of shops, at the end of which was Dealey's motor repair works. This family firm, started by Albert Stanley Dealey, was trading before the First World War as a cycle and motorcycle agency. In 1923 the firm moved to a showroom at 61 Gossoms End, with a new garage being built next door at 61A. The firm continued to be run by the sons after Albert died in 1961 and the firm finally closed in 1986.

The Crooked Billet

As we approach Billet Lane, a block of flats, built in the 1960s standing back from the road, is on the site of the Northchurch workhouse. The group of timber-framed cottages which were used for that purpose closed in 1832 and the inmates transferred to the Berkhamsted workhouse. On the opposite side of the track called Billet Lane stood the Crooked Billet public house. The old building was demolished in 1964 as part of a road-widening scheme, and the new public house, which had been built behind the existing one, was opened. Like many public houses it has now closed and the building is now a branch of the Majestic Wine Warehouse.

Billet Lane

In ancient times the River Bulbourne flowed from its source at Bulbourne Head to join the River Gade at Two Waters. From Norman times to the nineteenth century the water flow was strong enough to power two water mills in the town of Berkhamsted. However, following the construction of the Grand Junction Canal and the greater extraction of water from the chalk aquifer, the flow of water in the River Bulbourne has declined considerably. Where the Billet Lane crossed the river there was a ford with a roughly made wooden walkway for those who wished to keep their feet dry. In the background there is the parapet of the bridge which crosses the canal. Today at this point the river is in a culvert that originally continued through East's timber yard, now the site of the Stag Lane housing.

The Gasworks

On the other side of the canal was the gasworks, which moved from the town centre in 1906. Town gas, produced from coal, was generated on this site until 1959, but the two gasometers were used for storage until the whole of Britain was converted to natural gas between 1967 and 1977. The gasometers lasted for a while longer until they were demolished and the River Park Industrial Estate was created. Over the years the vegetation has grown substantially so the view from the canal is a much more tranquil scene.

The School Chapel and Castle Street, Berkhamsted.

Berkhamsted School Chapel

The principal buildings along Castle Street are those connected with Berkhamsted School. Founded in 1541 by Dean Incent, the original school house, the Old Hall, opened in 1544 at right angles to Castle Street and overlooks the churchyard of St Peter's. The lych-gate formed the main entrance into the school from Castle Street and gives entrance into the gravel quad. The foundation stone for the chapel was laid in 1894; it was the work of David Osborn, a local builder, and paid for by the headmaster, Dr Fry. The building was dedicated on 27 June 1895 and the interior imitated the design from the church of Santa Maria dei Miracoli in Venice. The architect was C. H. Rew.

Berkhamsted School Grass Quad

The chapel forms the east side of the grass quad with the cloister running alongside. During the First World War old Berkhamstedians joined the colours like numerous others from the public schools of the day. By the end of hostilities in 1918, of the 1,145 old boys who had served 184 were killed, 117 wounded and 244 had received gallantry awards. A subscription was organised and monies collected so that bronze tablets could be attached along the wall of the cloisters recording the names of those who fell in the First World War. In 1923/24 the school library was built where the low wall is in the foreground, which makes comparison photographs impossible.

The 'Sunken Cottages'

Before the canal was built, Castle Street followed the contour of the land towards the castle entrance. In 1798 the road was raised to facilitate the building of a bridge to cross the new canal. This meant that the entrance into cottages that lined the road were lower than the road surface, and the cottages became known locally as the 'sunken cottages'. Further down the road was the George & Dragon Temperance Hotel, established in 1879 with the support of Earl Brownlow. In the 1901 census it was run by William Saunders, who is described as a coffee house keeper, and Mrs E. A. Weeks continued the running of the hotel. The building was later purchased by Berkhamsted School and became known as St Georges.

Berkhamsted School Sanatorium

The historic row of sunken cottages was purchased by Berkhamsted School. They had become rather dilapidated by the time that they were demolished in 1963. In their place the school built a sanatorium for the boys, seen above. This has since been demolished and a new building, which is an arts centre above a dining room for the children, built.

Alsford's Timber Yard

When William Key finished working as a fencing contractor with the London to Birmingham Railway, he started a timber business in the High Street. The business moved to the top of Castle Street in 1913. Here he took over the wharf and coal yard that had previously been used by John Hatton, boatbuilder, coal and salt merchant. This allowed the timber to come directly by boat from Brentford to Key's Wharf. The timber sheds were used as mess rooms for the men of the Inns of Court Officer Training Corps during the First World War. In 1963 J. Alsford, another timber firm, purchased the site, but in 1994 modern canal side residences were built and are known as Alsford Wharf.

Costin's Boat Yard

With the coming of the Grand Junction Canal there was a need for a new type of boat for use on the canals. William Edward Costin set up his business on Castle Dock, which was where John Hatton once had his boat yard. The name Costin is well known in canal circles because he built boats for canal carriers such as Thomas Clayton and later for Fellows, Morton & Clayton, some of which were in regular use until the late 1960s. The boats were built under the protection of extensive sheds and were launched sideways due to the narrowness of the canal. The boats were sometimes used to give groups of local children a pleasure trip on the canal. A surviving memento of the J. Alsford timber yard is the 27-foot-high Indian totem pole made from Canadian red cedar by Henry Hunt, a Kwakiutl Indian from Vancouver Island, Canada, and which was erected in June 1970.

Grand Junction Canal

The locks on the Grand Junction Canal were built to accommodate wide boats of 14 feet, but most boats were built to a narrow gauge of 6 feet 10 inches so that two boats could be accommodated side by side. Initially they were horse drawn, but when they became motorised it was common for one which did not have a motor, the butty, to be towed by the one that did. These were often worked by a husband and wife team, and if they were owned by the family they were called 'Number Ones'. The husband usually steered the motor boat and the wife the butty. This pair is headed by number 105 *Quail*, owned by Fellows, Morton & Clayton Ltd, which was built at Uxbridge Dock in 1916.

Bridgewater Boats

With the demise of commercial carrying on the canals, the working boats were replaced, from the 1960s, by leisure craft. For people who could not afford or did not want to own a boat, companies that would hire a boat spread around the country. In Berkhamsted the firm was known as Bridgewater Boats and they hired out narrowboats for short periods of one or two weeks. The building on the canal wharf has been rebuilt following a serious fire that destroyed much of the original building. This is the last remaining canal wharf in Berkhamsted.

Cooper's Wharf

Continuing along the canal we reach the wharf and buildings of the Lower Works, which belonged to the firm of Cooper's, later Agr-Evo UK. This was where Cooper's dipping powder for sheep was manufactured until 1952, when the production ceased. This area was then used for the filling of aerosol sprays, which were used for the elimination of unwanted insect pests. The wharf would have been used in earlier days to receive the raw materials for the sheep dip powder. When the firm closed in 1997 the land was redeveloped for housing. Although the mooring bollards give the impression that boats still moor here, they now moor on the opposite, towpath side to gain refreshment at the local hostelry, the Rising Sun.

Girls Grammar School, Berkhamsted

Berkhamsted Girls School I

Berkhamsted Girls School was founded in 1888 and originally used the Bourne School building in the High Street. The school moved to the new purpose-built premises, when they opened in Kings Road, in 1902. The new school building was officially opened by Viscount Peel, a former speaker of the House of Commons. Although extended, the original building is still recognisably the same today.

Berkhamsted Girls School II

Viewed from the hill behind the school, it is obvious how extensively the school buildings have expanded across the site. Also, looking into the distance, to the opposite side of the valley, the large area of new housing can be seen. Extending from the castle to New Road at Northchurch, the Dellfield and Chiltern Park estates now cover a large area of former agricultural land to the north of the town.

Bridewell Lane

Looking down Kings Road, it is now hard to imagine that Bridewell Lane was so narrow. The bridewell stood on the right-hand side at the junction with the High Street. In 1894 the bridewell, together with an adjacent shop, was demolished to enable the construction of a new police station. This also allowed the lane to be widened as it had become a busy thoroughfare to Chesham. The police station has now closed, and the police officers have moved into part of the Civic Centre.

Lower Kings Road

The first post office was at 131 High Street, between Prince Edward Street and the Civic Centre, with Frederick Howard as the postmaster. He moved the office to new premises in Lower Kings Road in 1909; it remained there until it moved to the premises at the corner of Johns Well Lane in 1958. The building in Lower Kings Road has been replaced by the red-brick development called Claridge Court.

The Mantle Factory

In 1898 Henry George Hughes purchased land in Lower Kings Road and engaged James Honour & Son of Tring to build a factory in which he produced ladies' clothing called mantles. The building, although called the Bulbourne factory, was generally known as the mantle factory, and was sold to Corby, Palmer & Stewart in 1919, who expanded the business. During the period between the First and Second World Wars they employed between 750 and 800 people, mainly women, making women's and children's clothing. The business closed at Christmas 1969, following a takeover by Dennis Day Ltd, and the building was demolished and a car park established. Waitrose moved into its new premises in December 1996 behind part of the public car park.

Canal Fields Swimming Pool

In 1923 an open-air swimming pool opened in Canal Fields. As can be seen it was very popular, especially during the hot summer months. Facilities were fairly primitive but children had lots of fun and exercise. A new sports centre was built in 1990 on part of the playing fields at Gossoms End. These playing fields had formed part of the land that had once belonged to Lagley House. The facility in Canal Fields was bulldozed into the pool and the area grassed over. A skateboard park has been built in its place.

Castle Mill

By the side of the canal in Lower Kings Road, Berkhamsted's third mill was built, called Castle Mill. It was constructed in 1910 for a local farmer and corn merchant who lived at Broadway farm in Bourne End. The business was started by James Goodall Knowles and it was his son, Alfred G. Knowles, who took over the running of the business. The mill was equipped with a modern roller mill powered by either oil or steam. The business specialised in grinding a variety of grains, mainly for use in animal feeds. The building has now been redeveloped into flats, but the original walls were covered with a fresh layer of brick in order to blend with the additional housing built alongside.

Station Garage

Between Broadwater and the railway station stood the Station Garage, with B. Greene as the proprietor. It was advertised as a modern filling and repair station and was started before the Second World War. It later became the salesroom of Shaw & Kilburn, Vauxhall and Bedford dealers. The premises were demolished and housing built that recalls the early proprietor by being called Greenes Court.

Berkhamsted Railway Station

The London to Birmingham Railway came to Berkhamsted in 1837 and transformed passenger travel and freight to London. Initially there were only two lines, one to London and one to Birmingham. A new station was built in 1875, at which time the lines were doubled and an extensive goods yard was laid out where the car park is today. With the ease and speed of travel to and from London, Berkhamsted became a commuter town. It is unfortunate that when the line was built a part of the castle had to be demolished to accommodate it.

Cowper's Well

A short way along Rectory Lane, past the entrance into the cemetery, there is on the left-hand side of the road a small metal grating of little obvious significance. In earlier days, before the advent of piped water, most houses obtained their water supply from wells. This grating hides its history in that it was known as Cowper's Well. William Cowper, the poet, was born in 1731, the son of John Cowper, the rector of St Peter's church (1722–56), and the family lived in the rectory nearby. The family would have obtained their water from this source, which stood in the garden and, as can be seen, had a significant superstructure. When the adjacent land to the Rectory was sold in the 1960s, the rubble from building the Old Orchard was used to fill the well.

Rectory Lane Cemetery

The parish burial ground around St Peter's church was declared full and closed in 1855. The Countess of Bridgewater had previously given land between Three Close Lane and Rectory Lane for use as a detached burial ground in 1842. This is commemorated on a memorial against the wall on the south side of the cemetery. Further extensions were opened, one in 1894 and the other in 1921, and the photograph shows the later dedication. Many famous people are buried in cemeteries and within ours there are members of the Smith-Dorrien family, including General Sir Horace Lockwood Smith-Dorrien, the saviour of the British Expeditionary Force at Mons in 1914.

Clunbury Press

The Cooper's buildings in Manor Street housed a thriving printing department known as the Clunbury Press. They undertook a variety of commercial work in addition to the work for Cooper's. A new company amalgamating three firms, known as Cooper, McDougall & Robertson, was formed in 1925. There were several further changes in ownership, but the Clunbury Press continued with the printing of the firm's packaging and labels through to its eventual closure in the 1970s. Finally, the last owner, Agr-Evo, closed everything in 1997 and the site has now been turned into housing.

Cooper's Works

William Cooper was born in the Shropshire village of Clunbury. He trained as a veterinary surgeon and came to practise in Berkhamsted, where he found that there was an urgent call for a cure for sheep scab in the area. After some successful experiments he set up his first factory in Ravens Lane in 1852 and, as the business expanded, he accumulated the whole block of land between Manor Street and Ravens Lane for his enterprise. The raw materials for Cooper's Sheep Dipping Powder, including sulphur and arsenic, were brought in and the product sent out by canal. Following the Second World War the firm diversified into synthetic insecticides, and by 1973 the firm's products were marketed under the Wellcome name. With the closure of the site, the buildings were demolished and the land cleaned of the arsenic residues before new housing was built.

Photo.   Watercress St John's Well Lane, Berkhampstead

Bedford Watercress Beds

An important locally grown food during Victorian times was watercress. Originally grown in the bed of a chalk stream with little management, as the demand grew it was necessary to make purpose-built beds. Several generations of the Bedford family grew watercress initially at Dudswell and Northchurch, but in the 1901 census Harry Bedford was living at 2 St John's Well Lane in Berkhamsted and his beds were at the bottom of St John's Well Lane. They were supplied with a large quantity of fresh water from deep wells, which extracted the water from the chalk aquifer beneath. When Harry died, his eldest son Cecil took over and later his younger brother Dennis joined the enterprise. As the cost of production increased, it became uneconomical to produce watercress on the limited scale available in these beds, so the land was sold and the beds returned to become part of the River Bulbourne.

Castle Cottage

Berkhamsted Castle started to fall into disrepair after the last occupant, Cecily, Duchess of York, died in 1495. Elizabeth I gave the castle to Sir Edward Carey, who started the systematic demolition of the structures and from it built a new house, which was later called 'The Castle', but in reality was known as Berkhamsted Place. In the early Victorian censuses Colonel John Finch and his family lived in 'The Castle', and a keeper was living in The Castle House. From that time The Castle became a convenient source of materials which were used in other parts of the town. By 1900, when the National Monument Commission was examining historic buildings, the site was very overgrown. The present cottage was built in 1865 as a replacement to house a keeper to prevent further destruction of the walls and grounds. The bailey is now a large grassed area used for recreation by the local populace.

Castle Moat and Motte

The castle was built in the valley of the River Bulbourne and is in the Chiltern Hills. When the moats were excavated through the clay, the flints were collected and used to build the defensive structures and the curtain wall. When the moats were sufficiently deep, water would have emerged naturally from the chalk due to the water held by the surrounding hills being released. The local demand for water has been continually increasing so the level of the water in the chalk aquifer has fallen, so that it is now below the bottom level of the moat. It would now require significant rainfalls to refill the aquifer and allow the water to fill the moat.

Castle Moat

The rainfall in 1993 was sufficient to fill the moat to such an extent that the causeway from the modern entrance was flooded to a depth of a few inches. Obviously the level of the water on the walkway was not a deterrent to this hardy parent and children. Unfortunately water in the moat is now the exception rather than the norm, which is a pity as a moat full of water gives the castle a much greater visual impact than when it is full of vegetation.

A Nation of Shopkeepers

Napoleon is reported as saying that England was a nation of shopkeepers. In many respects he was right; in the early days open markets had been the way produce was bought and sold, but gradually the open market stall was replaced by the front of the family house becoming a shop. They became both a showroom and the retail outlet for the produce from the land, as well as for the goods produced by the shopkeepers. Shops were usually small family affairs, each specialising in one type of product. Henry Kingham & Sons ran a grocery business at 154 High Street; his shop was where the original Waitrose had been. L. & H. M. Gent ran a general store at 290 High Street which was next to the Methodist church. Both photographs were taken around the time of the Second World War and both show the pride that the shopkeepers had in their shops and produce.